MW01178556

ROBOTS AT WORK

WORLD
BOOK

www.worldbook.com

World Book, Inc.
180 North LaSalle Street
Suite 900
Chicago, Illinois 60601
USA

For information about other "Robots" titles, as well as other World Book print and digital publications, please go to www.worldbook.com or call 1-800-WORLDBK (967-5325).

For information about sales to schools and libraries, call 1-800-975-3250 (United States) or 1-800-837-5365 (Canada).

Library of Congress Cataloging-in-Publication Data for this volume has been applied for.

Robots
ISBN: 978-0-7166-4128-5 (set, hc.)

Robots at Work
ISBN: 978-0-7166-4133-9 (hc.)

Also available as:
ISBN: 978-0-7166-4143-8 (e-book)

Printed in China by RR Donnelley, Guangdong Province
1st printing May 2019

Staff

Writer: William D. Adams

Executive Committee

President
Geoff Broderick

Vice President, Finance
Donald D. Keller

Vice President, Marketing
Jean Lin

Vice President, International
Maksim Rutenberg

Vice President, Technology
Jason Dole

Director, Human Resources
Bev Ecker

Editorial

Director, New Print
Tom Evans

Managing Editor
Jeff De La Rosa

Editor
William D. Adams

Librarian
S. Thomas Richardson

Manager, Contracts and Compliance (Rights and Permissions)
Loranne K. Shields

Manager, Indexing Services
David Pofelski

Digital

Director, Digital Product Development
Erika Meller

Digital Product Manager
Jon Wills

Graphics and Design

Senior Art Director
Tom Evans

Senior Visual Communications Designer
Melanie Bender

Media Editor
Rosalia Bledsoe

Manufacturing/ Production

Manufacturing Manager
Anne Fritzinger

Production Specialist
Curley Hunter

Proofreader
Nathalie Strassheim

Contents

Terms defined in the glossary are in type **that looks like this** on their first appearance on any spread (two facing pages).

Dull, Dirty, Dangerous

Imagine if you worked on an assembly line and had to put the same two parts together over and over again. Or imagine you had to work in a dusty mine where rock falls were common. That doesn't sound too great, right? Fortunately, robots do many of these jobs for us. And with today's advances in robotics technology, they are poised to do even more.

Robots have been put to work in dull, dirty, and dangerous jobs. Robots are great at putting the same two pieces together in an assembly line, over and over, day after day. They can do jobs that people find gross, or that are in conditions that might make them sick. They can also be sent into areas that are too expensive—or

Dull duties
Does stamping the date on thousands of tuna cans sound like your dream job? Probably not! Robots do not mind such boring tasks, and they can do them quickly with few mistakes.

impossible—to make safe for humans. As robotics technology improves, robots are also being entrusted with delicate tasks that require more control than human hands can provide.

In this book, you will read about robots that work for people. You'll learn about the different types of **industrial robots.** You'll also get to meet some of the hard-working 'bots that help us people do some of the dullest and dirtiest, and most dangerous and delicate jobs.

Dangerous work
Robots can do jobs such as welding that carry a risk of injury, keeping human workers at a safe distance.

Industrial Robots

Industrial robots work in factories to help make many of the products we use every day. They come in many different sizes, but they are all in some way bolted in place. Work comes to them from conveyor devices.

Different industrial robots use different combinations of **rotary joints** and **translational joints.** In a rotary joint, one part twists or turns in relation to another, just like a human knee or wrist. In a translational joint, one part extends out or moves along a track. The angle between the two parts doesn't change, but one part moves in or out (or up or down) in relation to the other part.

An industrial robot's combination of joints is laid out to give it a **work envelope** suitably sized for the job it is supposed to do. Most industrial robots have at least three joints so they can have a large, flexible work envelope.

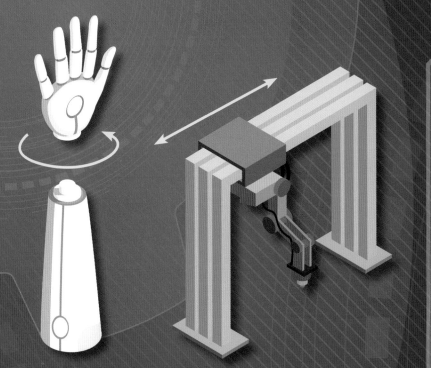

HELLO, MY NAME IS:

Unimate

Unimate was the first **industrial robot.** It made its debut in 1961 at a U.S. automobile assembly plant. Unimate was a type of robot called a spherical robot because its one **translational joint** and two **rotational joints** were arranged to create a shell-like **work envelope** around it. Today, most industrial robots are of other types.

Unimate was the first practical robot to make a dent in pop culture. It performed fun demonstrations for the public and made appearances on television.

AUTONOMY

MEDIUM

Robots are driven by more powerful computers today, enabling greater autonomy, but at the time, Unimate was a major breakthrough.

SIZE

Unimate was a hefty 'bot, weighing 2,700 pounds (1,200 kilograms).

MAKER

The American company Unimation created Unimate.

GOOD CO-WORKER

Though industrial robots took time to catch on, factory managers—and even the workers—where they were installed quickly grew to appreciate them. Unimation avoided selling to companies that were laying off employees to avoid resentment from other workers.

Articulated Robots
(Robotic Arms)

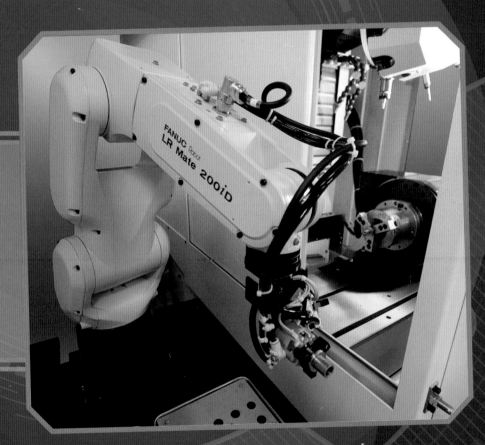

Articulated robots are the workhorses of the **industrial robot** world. They usually have three or more **rotary joints,** creating a large, three-dimensional **work envelope** in which they can reach things to do their jobs.

Articulated robots come in all shapes and sizes. They can be fitted with different **actuators** to

Armed and ready
An articulated robot is a robotic "arm" that can bend, twist, and reach to do its job.

Articulated robots are used for all kinds of jobs. These articulated robots are painting cars.

do many different industrial tasks. They weld, move things, grind metal, or put parts together. Some even work with food!

Some articulated robots take manufactured goods and pack them onto pallets for easy shipment. A lot of material is moved on standard shipping pallets, which are 48 inches by 40 inches (122 centimeters by 102 centimeters).

Cartesian and Gantry Robots

Think of a claw crane game, where the claw can travel front-to-back, side-to-side, and finally down to try to grab a prize. Some **industrial robots** work much the same way. They have three **translational joints,** and sometimes work overhead. Fortunately for the factories that use them, their **effectors** are much more reliable than the claws of claw crane games!

Cartesian robots have three translational joints, all at 90-degree angles from one another, that allow parts of the robot to slide on a track. These robots are simple and effective, but their design allows them only to pick up smaller objects.

A gantry robot is similar to a Cartesian robot, but with an additional track over one or both horizontal axes to support the robot's weight. This arrangement allows for fine-tuned movements and larger loads. Gantry robots are often large and mounted high above the factory floor.

Gantry robots are like robotic cranes. In this warehouse, a gantry robot (shown at the top of the photograph) is used to stack containers.

SCARA

Circuit boards are an essential part of everyday life, including robots themselves! As the need for circuit boards exploded and parts got smaller and smaller, manufacturers came up with ways to speed up production. One way is to assemble parts of them with a kind of **industrial robot** called

Sketchy SCARA
SCARA robots are known for their pinpoint control. This 'bot fancies itself a bit of an artist.

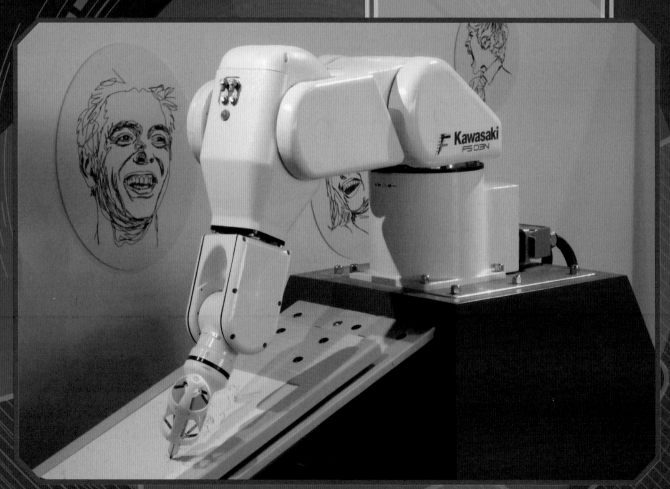

a *selective compliance assembly robot arm* (SCARA). SCARA's have two **rotary joints** that rotate on the same axis and one **translational joint** that raises and lowers the **effector.** This gives them a flatter **work envelope** than other types of industrial robots. But SCARA's have pinpoint control over this area, making them perfect for working on such things as circuit boards.

SCARA's are great for tasks that require only limited motions. Such tasks include packaging or handling small items.

Parallel Link Robots

Parallel link robots are a strange-looking type of **industrial robot.** Three or four arms, each with a **rotational joint actuator** at the base, all attach to a single **effector.**

Because the arms are attached together this way, the robot has a small **work envelope.** Why attach the arms together? Parallel link robots can move small items inside their work envelopes with amazing speed and precision. For example, they can take objects scattered on a conveyor belt and stack them neatly for packaging. While moving the objects, they can rotate them so that they are all facing the same direction.

Parallels link robots can sort and stack parts at lightning speed.

ROBOT
CHALLENGE

Working With People

Industrial robots can be dangerous coworkers. They operate with a lot of force and only sense changes to the things they are working on. A person wandering into an industrial robot's **work envelopes** could get clobbered by its swinging arm. Engineers have come up with different solutions to keep workers safe. Robots are often put in cages, not to keep the 'bots in, but to keep people from getting too close to them while they are working.

Be safe
Human workers use caution and wear safety equipment near an industrial robot.

Most robots also have a training mode, where the motors operate more slowly and with less power. This allows human programmers to enter a robot's cage to see if it's performing a new routine correctly.

HELLO, MY NAME IS:

FANUC's lights-out factories

The easiest way to make sure **industrial robots** don't hurt people is to keep them separate. The best way to do this is not to build cages, but to have no people work in the factory at all. The robot manufacturer FANUC has 22 factories at its headquarters in Japan, all of which operate with very little human intervention. Fewer than five people are at each factory at any one time, and several more monitor them from afar.

AUTONOMY

HIGH |||||||||||||||||||||

The factories need little input from humans. About 80% of the manufacturing process is completed by machines. Engineers do the wiring. The factories can go for up to 30 days without human input. People deliver raw materials to them. The robotic factories work until they run out of raw materials or space to store the new robots.

LIGHTS OUT

FANUC's factories rarely have people in them, so the lights are turned off to save energy. The robots work in the dark!

PRODUCTION

Over 2,000 robots can produce more than 250,000 robots every year.

MAKER

FANUC

Cobots

Industrial robot manufacturers are also creating robots that are better coworkers. These collaborative robots, also known as **cobots,** have **sensors** to spot humans and may slow down, stop, or change their movement when they are near. But more than that, cobots are designed to work with humans. Humans even train

Better together
Cobots are robots designed to work well with humans. Sawyer, a cobot by the American company Rethink Robotics, has video-screen eyes that show human coworkers where its attention is focused.

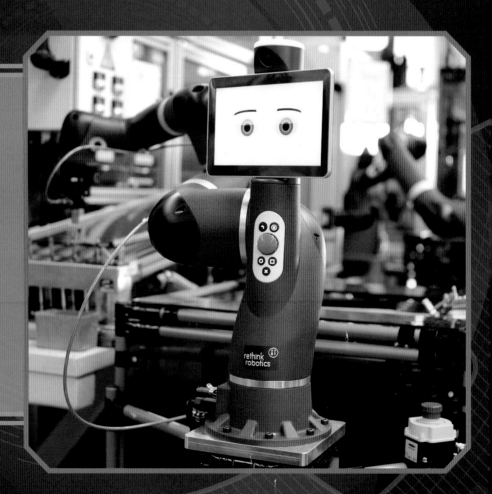

some of them to perform tasks by guiding them through the movements needed to complete the task. These features make cobots safer, more flexible, and more useful to more kinds of industries and small businesses. Soon, cobots may be working alongside people in many factories, making their jobs easier and more interesting by doing the difficult or boring parts.

AGV's

Automated guided vehicles (AGV's) move things around factories and warehouses. Though they are not usually considered **industrial robots,** they often work closely with them. Towing vehicles—also called tuggers—can push or pull carts loaded with pallets or raw materials to different locations. They can be many cars long and haul tens of thousands of pounds or kilograms. **Automated** forklifts work just like their crewed counterparts. They slide long metal forks under a pallet packed with merchandise to pick it up and move it to a different location. They can reach many yards or meters to pick up or set down pallets on high racks.

Tuggers (robotic towing vehicles) haul materials and products around factories and warehouses.

Automated forklifts lift pallets and shelve products.

Technological Unemployment

Are robots getting too good at our jobs? Some people worry that improvements in robotics, **automation,** and **artificial intelligence (AI)** will put many people out of work. For instance, if self-driving car technology is perfected, fleets of **autonomous** taxis would put out of business not only cab drivers, but also many independent repair shops and gas stations.

Some jobs (such as that of taxi driver) may be completely wiped out by automation. But most jobs have parts that can't be automated easily. Robots and AI might do the boring parts of a job while people do the parts that require greater flexibility. In this way, the same number of people can do more work with the help of robots and automation. There will also be more robot engineer, programmer, and mechanic jobs as the use of robots in workplaces grows.

Humans need not apply
Human workers are nowhere to be seen in this photograph of a factory where jobs are done by robots.

Mining Robots

Mining is perfectly suited to robotic **automation:** it's often dull, dirty, and dangerous all at once. Add to that another D: distant. Many mines are far from where people live. People who work in these mines often have to live on-site, which is boring for them and expensive for the company. Automating mining processes means that fewer people have to be transported to or live at the mine site.

Robot miner
An automated loader scoops rock at a mine.

For aboveground mines, robots can use **Global Positioning System (GPS)** to find where they are. But GPS doesn't work underground, and many other types of **sensors** can't survive the harsh conditions found in underground mines. Some inventors are using rugged cameras combined with **software** that mimics the brains of such animals as rats to create robots that can **autonomously** find their way around harsh, changing underground mine environments.

Valuable minerals can be found in locations even more remote than faraway underground mines, such as the bottom of the ocean and asteroids in space. If mining could be completely automated, such sites might become profitable to mine.

HELLO, MY NAME IS:

Caterpillar 793F CMD self-driving dump truck

One of the largest land vehicles doesn't have to have a driver. The Caterpillar 793F CMD is a huge mining dump truck that can be programmed to run **autonomously.** The self-driving truck doesn't need to take any breaks other than to refuel or repair, so it's 20% more productive than the human-driven version. So far, these autonomous trucks have hauled more than 400 million tons (360 million metric tons) of rock and ore without a human injury.

AUTONOMY

HIGH

This titanic truck will pull up next to the digging machines, drive away when its bed is full, and dump the material at a dump site, all while avoiding other trucks and people.

MAKER

The American company Caterpillar makes a wide variety of self-driving dump trucks. Their systems can even be fitted onto competitor's trucks!

SIZE

375,000 pounds (170,000 kilograms), 21 ½ feet (6.5 meters) tall, 45 feet (13.7 meters) long

CAPACITY

250 tons (227 metric tons)—more than a blue whale, the largest animal ever!

Robotic Farming

Many parts of farming are already **automated.** Beginning in the late 1990's, many tractors and combines have been fitted with **GPS** receivers, allowing farmers to guide them with less effort. Because **robotic vision** systems and other **sensors,** such as **lidar,** have improved, engineers

An easy row to hoe
An automated tractor might allow a farmer to plant, fertilize, and harvest a field without ever setting foot in it.

are working towards creating driverless tractors and other equipment. Such farming activities as planting and harvesting must take place in very short windows of time. Robotic farm equipment could work 24 hours a day if need be to get the job done.

In addition to self-driving farm equipment, robotics will help farmers in other ways. Advances in robotic vision will soon allow robotic tractor attachments to identify weeds and spray them with pesticide. This will limit the amount of pesticide needed in a field, reducing costs to the farmer and harm to the environment.

Rowbot

Farmers grow corn in long rows. The plants get tall quickly, so tractors can't drive over it shortly after it has been planted. Corn plants needs fertilizer at certain times throughout the year, but sometimes the rows are already too tall for farmers to fertilize them. A robot called Rowbot might be able to help. It's narrow enough to fit between the rows of corn. It will use **robotic vision** to analyze the quality of the corn and apply fertilizer if it is needed.

AUTONOMY

HIGH

Rowbot will use **sensors,** such as **GPS** and **lidar,** to keep track of its location as it moves through the corn.

WIN-WIN-WIN

By spraying fertilizer right at plants' roots at just the right times, Rowbot will allow farmers to use less fertilizer, saving them money and reducing harm to the environment, while still improving crop yield.

MAKER

The American company Rowbot Systems LLC is developing the 'bot.

SIZE

2 feet (60 centimeters) wide, narrow enough to fit between rows of corn, which are usually planted 30 inches (76 centimeters) apart

Automated Fruit Harvesting

If you think about it, picking fruit is hard to do. You have to identify fruit on a tree or bush, figure out whether it's ripe or not, and then gently pick the ripe fruit without damaging it or the plant. Humans get the hang of it pretty quickly, but it is a very difficult task for a robot to master.

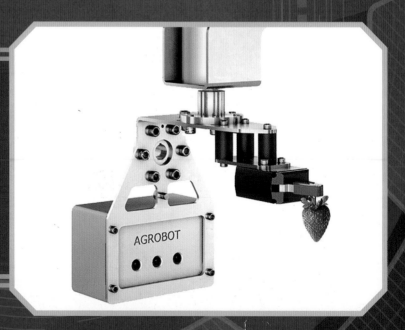

Low-hanging fruit
A strawberry harvester does not have to touch the fruit. It simply grasps and cuts the long stem.

If this job is so hard for a robot to do, why are engineers trying to get robots to do it? Picking fruit is exhausting work. It needs to be done at certain times of year. It's hard to predict how many workers will be needed, and when they will be needed. Because of these difficulties, fruit sometimes rots before it can get picked.

Engineers are working on robots with computer learning systems to figure out what they should be picking. Some designs use delicate grippers to grab the piece of fruit and pull it off the tree or bush. Others suck the fruit up with a vacuum.

Self-Driving Trucks

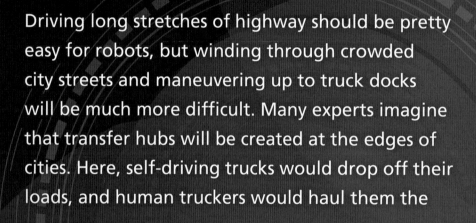

Long-haul trucking is a dull job. Most people who try it quit in their first year, so transportation companies have a hard time finding enough drivers. Self-driving trucks could revolutionize shipping.

Driving long stretches of highway should be pretty easy for robots, but winding through crowded city streets and maneuvering up to truck docks will be much more difficult. Many experts imagine that transfer hubs will be created at the edges of cities. Here, self-driving trucks would drop off their loads, and human truckers would haul them the

Self-driving trucks could revolutionize the transportation industry.

last several miles or kilometers to stores, restaurants, and factories. This arrangement would make truck driving a better job. Last-mile truckers could spend more time at home and work more regular shifts.

This is just one possibility for the future of self-driving trucks. Instead, a person might remotely pilot a truck through difficult parts of its trip, such as through crowded streets or construction zones. Or **automated drones** may bring small cargo directly to people (see pages 44-45).

Self-driving short-hauler
The Swedish company Volvo Trucks is developing an electric, self-driving truck called Vera. Vera is designed for short hauls, such as moving freight in a freight yard.

inspection Robots

Remote-controlled vehicles are already used to inspect buildings, bridges, and other pieces of infrastructure. Robot-like devices can check the status of equipment in places where humans cannot go. These machines check gas pipes; electrical lines; and heating, ventilation, and air conditioning ducts. Although these machines look like robots, they have no **autonomy.**

Inspector Snake
Researchers test a snakelike inspection robot.

High-wire act
This remote-controlled inspection device climbs up and down bridge cables, looking for damage.

But soon, some of these devices may be **automated.** For example, small fleets of autonomous **drones** may fly around a region, constantly inspecting bridges, overpasses, and tunnels. In many ways, robots are better inspectors than humans are. Once they are trained on what to look for, they will almost always find it if it's there. They can detect cracks or imperfections too small for human eyes to see.

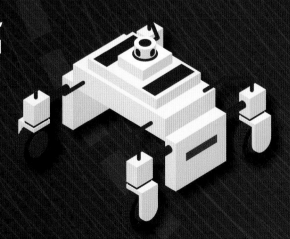

HELLO, MY NAME IS:

Air-Cobot

Airplanes go through many checks to make sure that they are safe to fly. These checks are important, but they take a lot of time. It's also hard for people to see problems with airplanes that could lead to disaster, such as tiny cracks. Makers of the Air-Cobot hope to speed up and improve the most common checks. Cameras and **sensors** on this wheeled robot could detect potential problems with an airplane and let mechanics know about them.

AUTONOMY

HIGH

Air-Cobot will drive out to the planes to perform scheduled inspections. It will alert mechanics when it has found a problem with an airplane. When it is running low on power or needs maintenance itself, it will return to its hangar.

SIZE

57 x 31 x 47 inches (145 x 80 x 120 centimeters)

MAKER

The French company AKKA Technologies is developing Air-Cobot.

WORKS WELL WITH OTHERS!

Air-Cobot is designed to work in busy airports. It will use sensors to detect and avoid obstacles, such as luggage carts and workers, while performing or traveling to an inspection. Air-Cobots will store their reports and images in a shared database, allowing them to compare damage and wear among planes. Engineers plan to partner Air-Cobots with autonomous **drones** to check the upper parts of airplanes.

Delivery Robots

Soon, walking, rolling, and flying robots will be making deliveries to homes and businesses. **Autonomous drones** may deliver small packages to both sparsely populated country areas and crowded cities much more quickly and cheaply than human-driven road vehicles. Other companies are creating wheeled delivery robots. These robots are designed to travel on sidewalks at a fast walking speed to deliver food or other packages. When one of these robots reaches its destination, the person who made the order unlocks it with a code or a smartphone. Another company is creating a two-legged robot that could easily hop curbs and climb stairs to make deliveries in crowded cities.

Starship ships fish and chips
Starship is a small robot that makes food deliveries by traveling on sidewalks.

Glossary

actuator a device, such as a motor, that provides movement to a robot.

articulated robot a robot that uses rotary joints. The most common articulated robots are armlike industrial robots.

artificial intelligence (AI) the ability of a computer system to process information in a manner similar to human thought or to exhibit humanlike behavior.

automation the use of machines to perform tasks that require decision making.

automated guided vehicle (AGV) a mobile robot that follows wires, tape, or markers to move items or people around.

autonomy the degree to which a robot can make decisions without input from a human operator to achieve a goal.

collaborative robot (cobot) an industrial robot designed to work closely with people and share workspaces with them.

drone an uncrewed aerial vehicle. Most drones are piloted remotely, but some are autonomous.

effector the part of the robot's body, such as a wheel or a gripper, that is moved by an actuator and interacts with the environment to perform an action.

Global Positioning System (GPS) a worldwide navigation system that uses radio signals broadcast by satellites.

industrial robot a robot that works in a factory to help create a product.

lidar a sensor that uses beams of light to judge the distance of objects. The word *lidar* comes from *li*ght *d*etection and *r*anging.

robotic vision the use of cameras and computers to recognize patterns and objects in images.

rotary joint a type of joint in which one end rotates or twists in relation to the other.

sensor a device that takes in information from the outside world and translates it into code.

software a general term for computer programs. A computer program is mostly made up of a sequence of instructions. The instructions tell a computer what to do and how to do it.

translational joint a type of joint in which one part extends out or moves along a track.

work envelope the area in which an industrial robot can reach and manipulate objects with its effector.

Additional Resources

Faust, Daniel. *Manufacturing Robots.* New York: PowerKids, 2017.

Graham, Ian. *You Wouldn't Want to Live Without Robots!* New York: Franklin Watts, 2019.

Higgins, Nadia. *Factory Robots.* Mankato, MN: Amicus Ink, 2018.

Smibert, Angie. *Building Better Robots.* North Mankato, MN: 12-Story Library, 2017.

Bristol Robotics Laboratory
   http://www.brl.ac.uk/default.aspx

IEEE - Robots
   https://robots.ieee.org/

Learn About Robots - Industrial Robots
   https://www.learnaboutrobots.com/industrial.htm

Rowbot
   https://www.rowbot.com/

Acknowledgments

Cover: © Kirill Makarov, Shutterstock
4-5   © Noppawat Tom Charoensinphon, Getty Images; © Praphan Jampala, Shutterstock
6-7   © Josep Curto, Shutterstock
8-9   National Institute of Standards and Technology; © Gamma-Keystone/Getty Images
10-11   © FANUC; © Andrei Kholmov, Shutterstock
12-13   © Tecnowey
14-15   Public Domain; Hirata Robotics GmbH (licensed under CC BY-SA 3.0 DE)
16-17   Humanrobo (licensed under CC BY-SA 3.0)
18-19   © Ndoeljindoel/Shutterstock
20-21   © Alexander Tolstykh, Shutterstock
22-23   © Rethink Robotics
24-25   AGV Expert JS (licensed under CC BY-SA 3.0); Carmenter (licensed under CC BY-SA 4.0)
26-27   © Nataliya Hora, Shutterstock
28-29   © Tomas Westermark, Boliden; © Christian Sprogoe Photography/Rio Tinto
30-31   © Caterpillar
32-33   © CNH Industrial America; © Ruslan Ivantsov, Shutterstock
34-35   © Rowbot Systems
36-37   © Agrobot
38-39   © Otto; © Volvo Trucks
40-41   Charles Buynak, U.S. Air Force; Doug Thaler (licensed under CC BY-SA 4.0)
42-43   © AKKA Technologies
44-45   © Starship Technologies

Index